162 Traditional and

Cornwall ... for

St ... ts

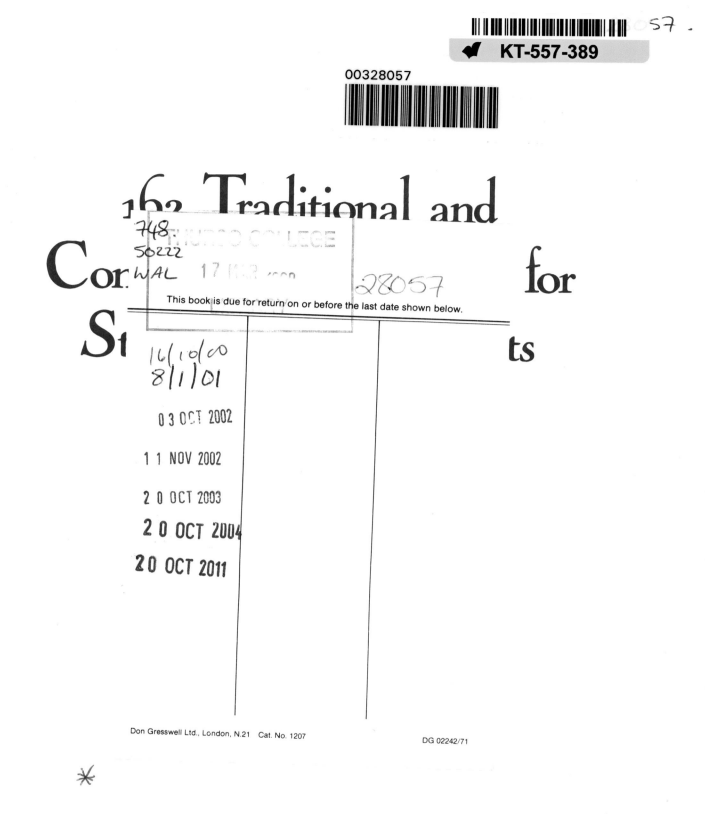

DOVER PUBLICATIONS, INC.
New York

Copyright © 1974, 1976, 1978, 1980 and 1991 by Joel Wallach.
All rights reserved under Pan American and International Copyright
Conventions.

Published in Canada by General Publishing Company, Ltd., 30 Lesmill
Road, Don Mills, Toronto, Ontario.
Published in the United Kingdom by Constable and Company, Ltd., 3
The Lanchesters, 162–164 Fulham Palace Road, London W6 9ER.

162 Traditional and Contemporary Designs for Stained Glass Projects, first
published by Dover Publications, Inc., in 1991, is a new selection of
illustrations from four books published by The Glass Works Press, San
Diego: *Patterns & Designs in Stained Glass*, 1974; *Patterns & Designs in Stained
Glass—2*, 1976; *Patterns & Designs in Stained Glass—3*, 1978; and *Beginning
Stained Glass Patterns—Book 2*, 1980.

DOVER *Pictorial Archive* SERIES

Manufactured in the United States of America
Dover Publications, Inc., 31 East 2nd Street, Mineola, N. Y. 11501

Library of Congress Cataloging-in-Publication Data

162 traditional and contemporary designs for stained glass projects / edited
by Joel Wallach.
     p.   cm.—(Dover pictorial archive series)
  ISBN 0-486-26928-0 (pbk.)
   1. Glass painting and staining—Patterns. I. Wallach, Joel.
II. Title: One hundred sixty-two traditional and contemporary designs
for stained glass projects.   III. Title: One hundred and sixty-two traditional and contemporary designs for stained glass projects.   IV. Series.
TT298.A16   1991
748.5′022′2—dc20   91-4956
                                                      CIP

Publisher's Note

RANGING FROM TRADITIONAL Victorian and Edwardian designs to contemporary abstract and nature-inspired forms, this book is a tour of the palette of styles available to today's stained glass artisan. This collection of 162 stained glass designs by various artists proceeds generally from abstract motifs to flowers (including roses, poppies, sunflowers, morning glories, daffodils and irises) and thence to birds (including a crane, a partridge, a parrot, a hummingbird, a swan and a gull) and scenic compositions. The craftsperson will also find here useful representations of bamboo, grapes, suns, shells, a sailboat and a fleur-de-lys.

From the severely geometric to the exuberantly florid, this is an excellent comprehensive one-volume anthology of patterns for use in stained glass. The designs in this book, covering a wide range of styles and shapes, are well suited to a number of crafts applications including mobiles, ornaments, lightcatchers, windows, mirrors, candle shelters, panels, lampshades and fanlights. All of the designs can be reduced or enlarged as necessary using easily available photostatic equipment.

This book is intended as a supplement to stained glass instruction books (such as *Stained Glass Craft* by J. A. F. Divine and G. Blachford, Dover Publications, Inc., 0-486-22812-6). All materials needed, including general instructions and tools for beginners, can usually be purchased from local craft and hobby stores listed in your Yellow Pages.

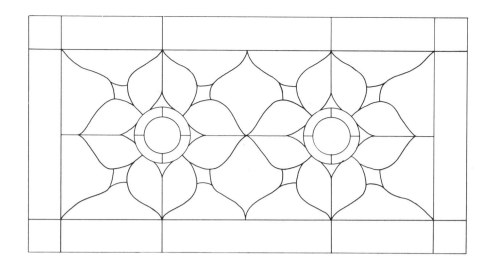

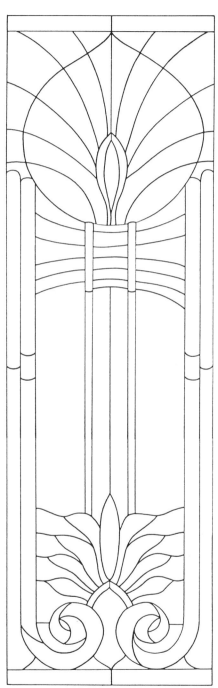

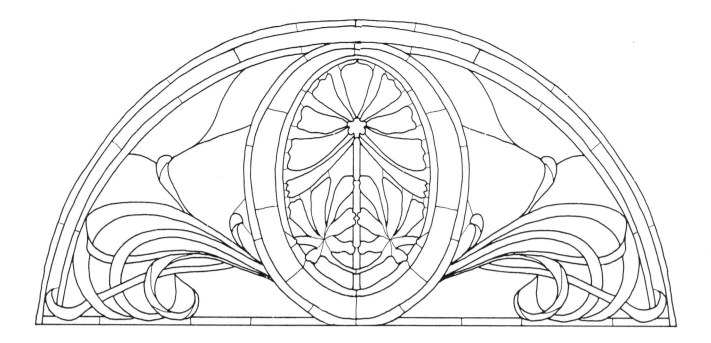

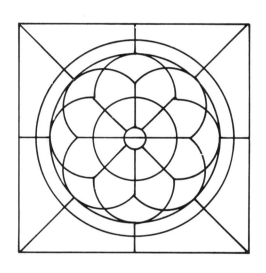

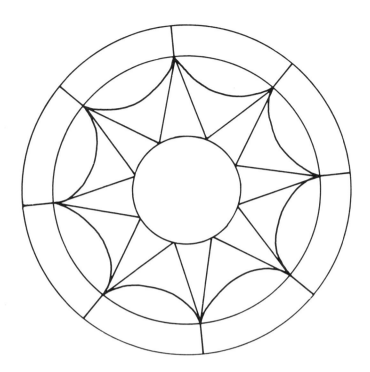

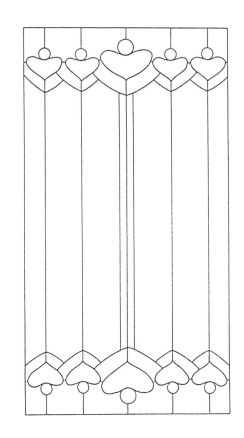

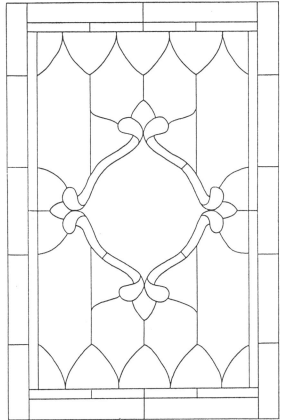

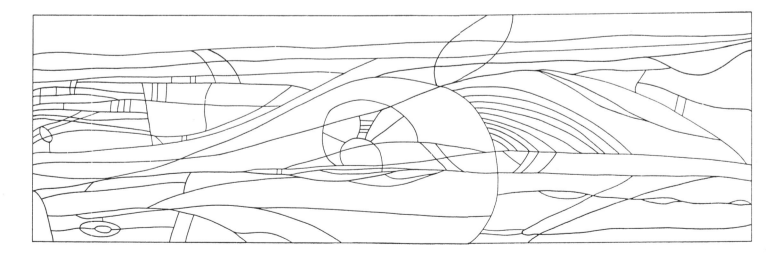

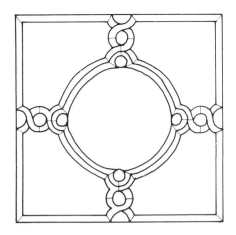

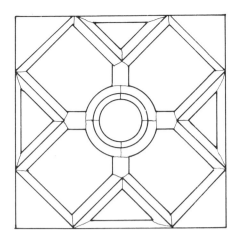

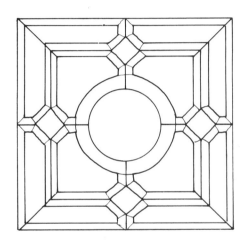

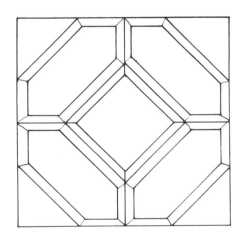

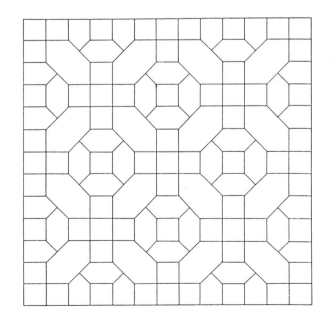

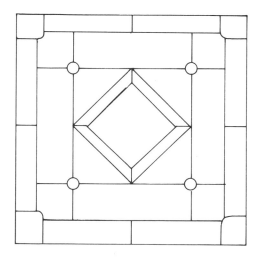

9

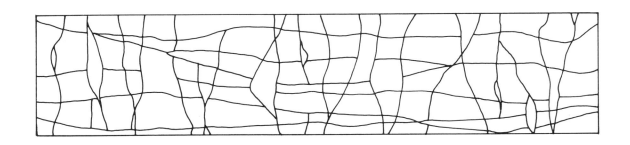

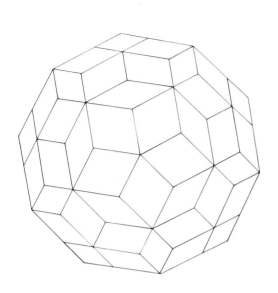

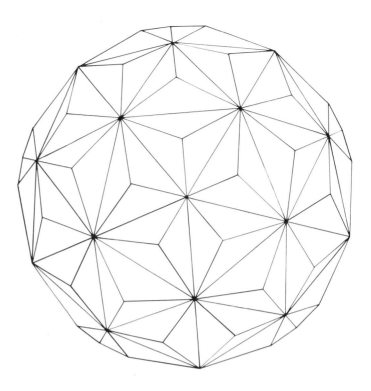

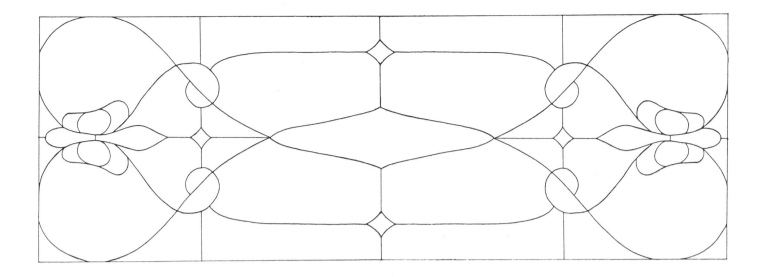

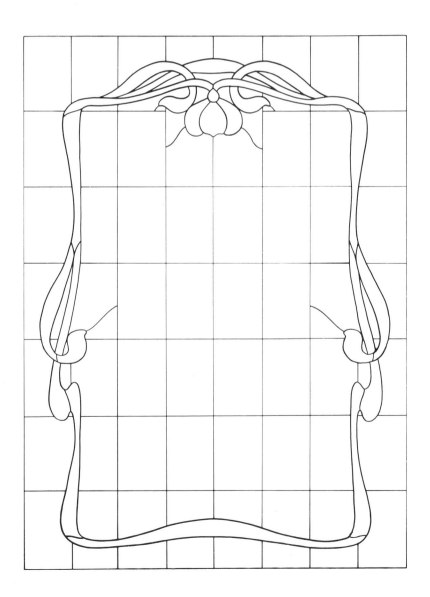

15

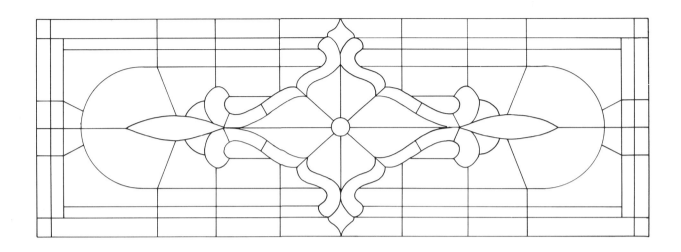

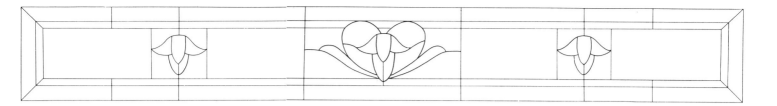

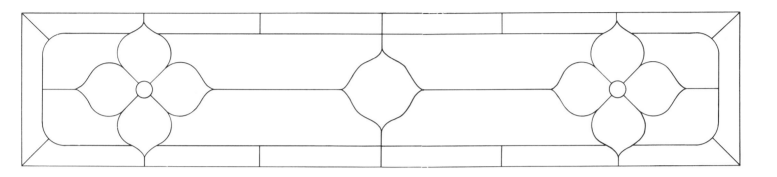

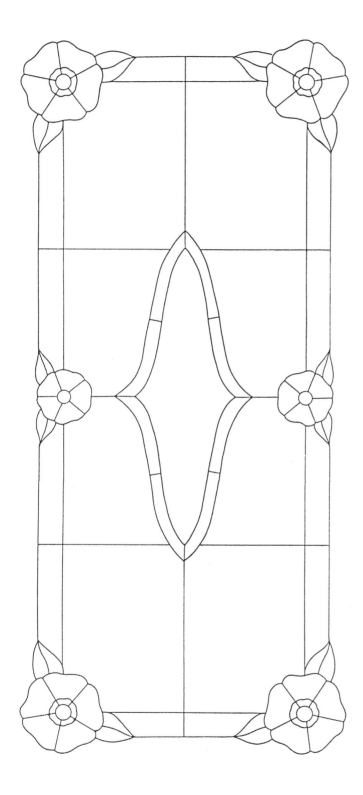

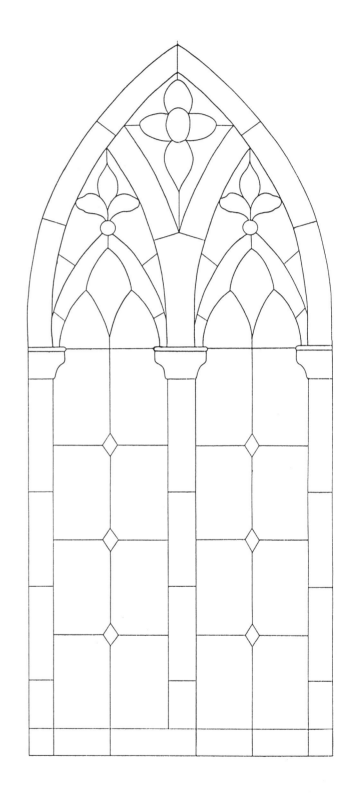

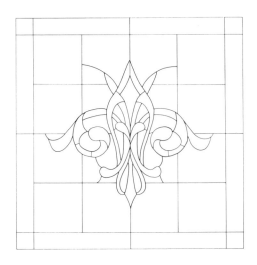

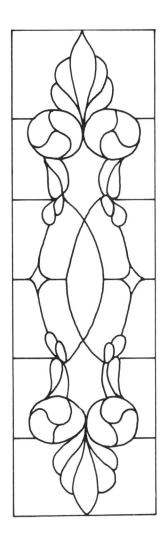

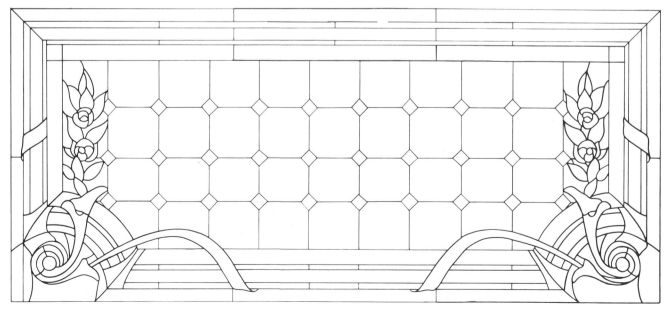

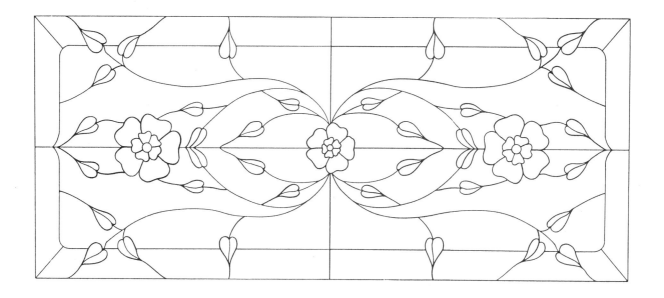

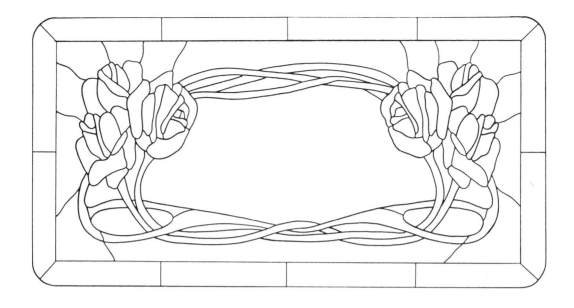

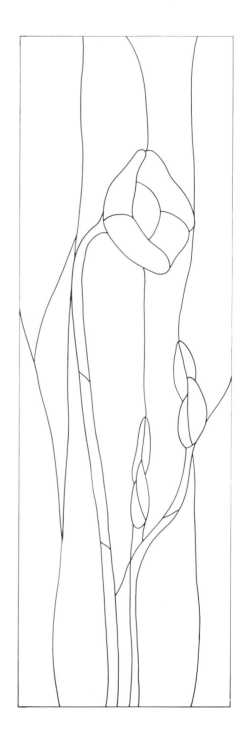

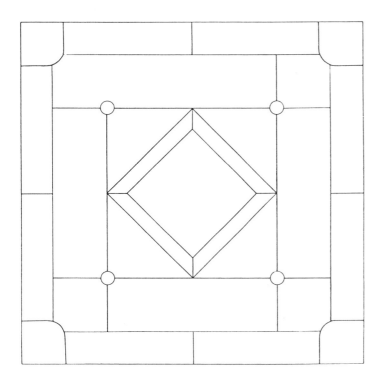

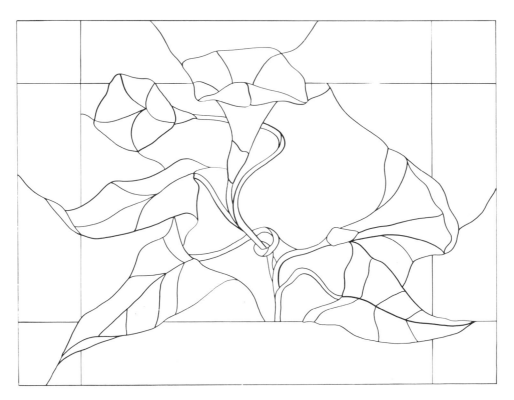

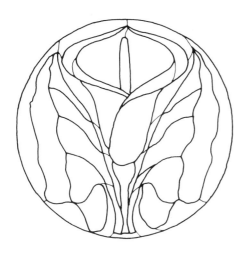

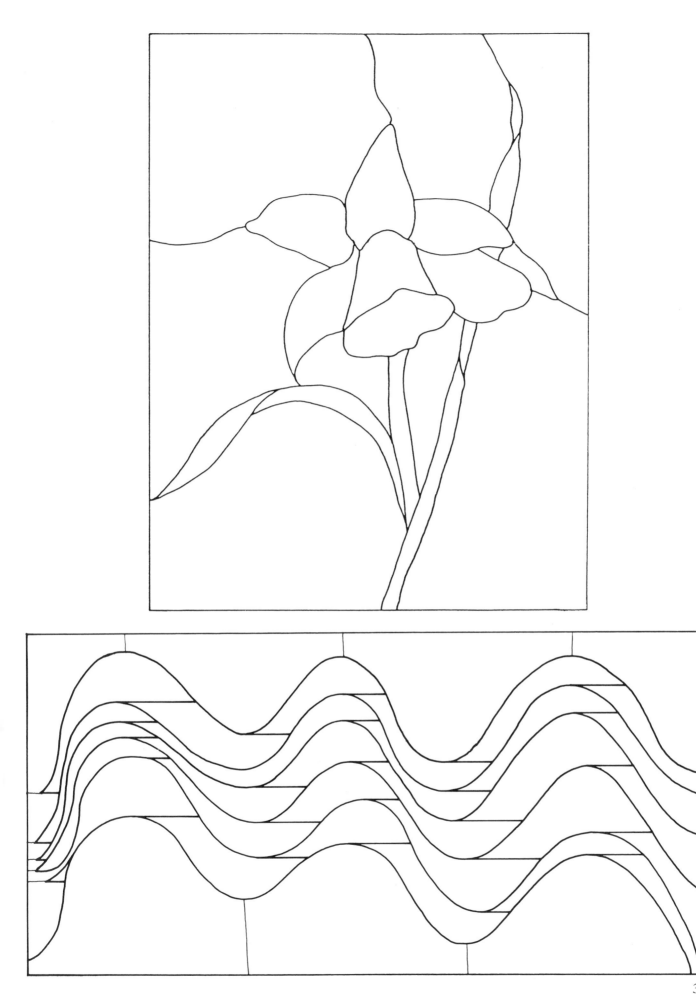

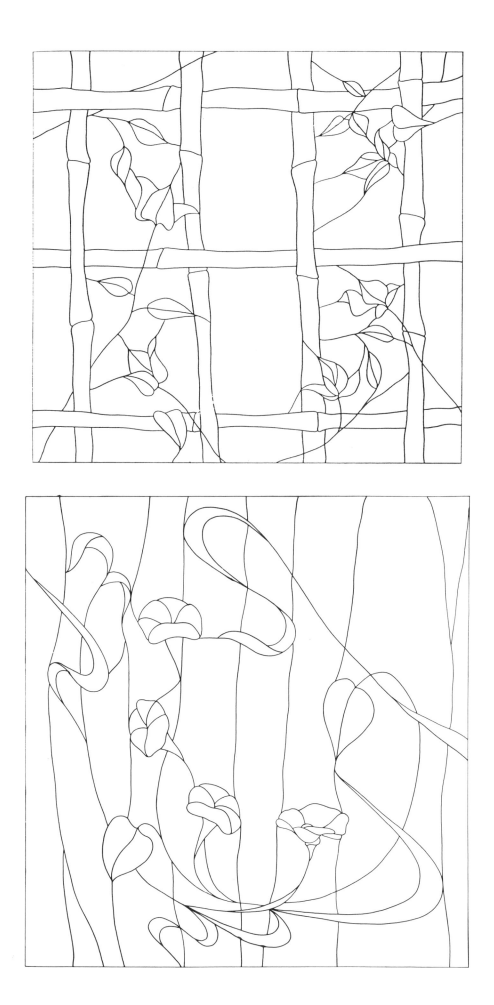

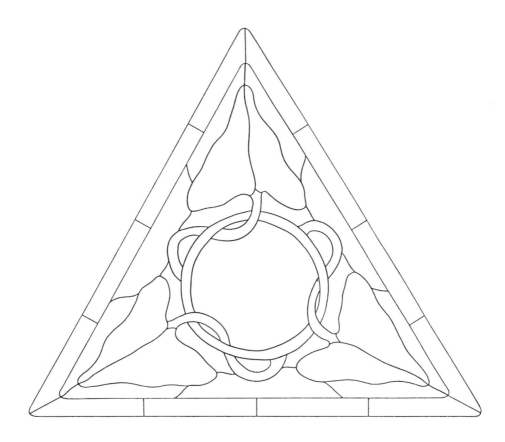

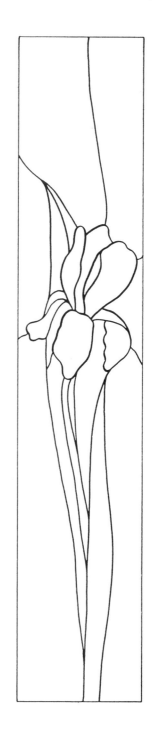

41

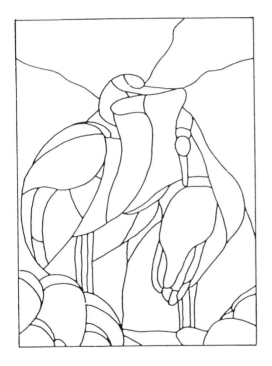

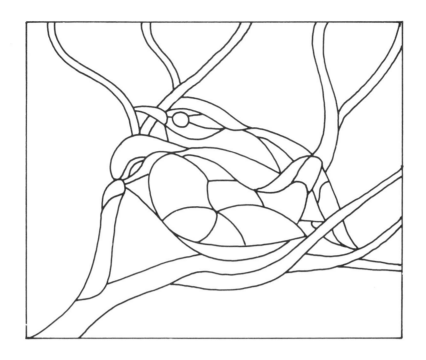

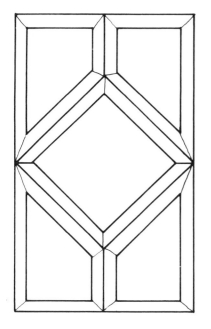
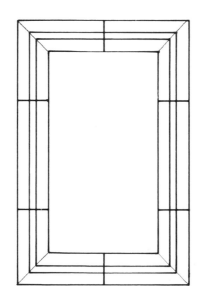
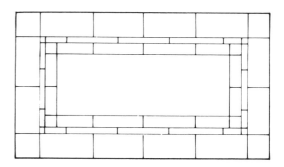
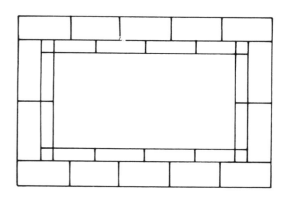

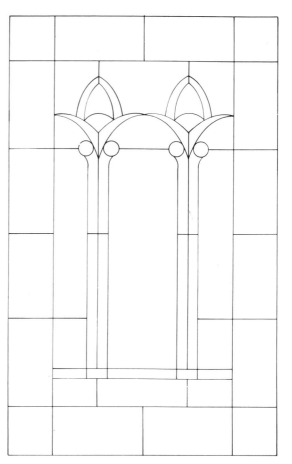

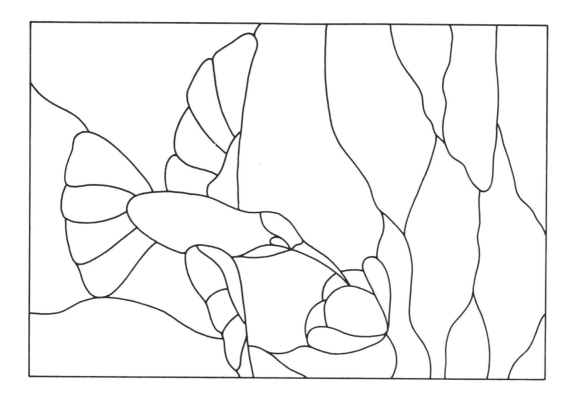

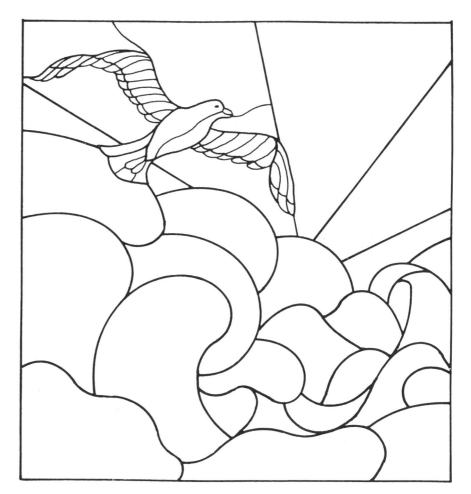

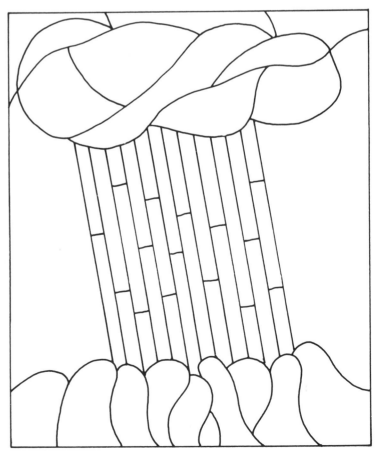

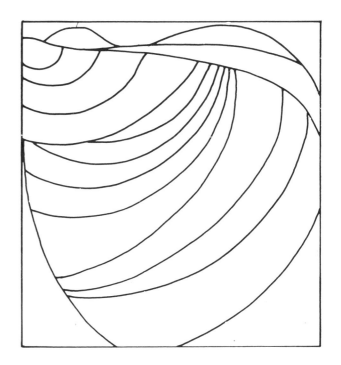

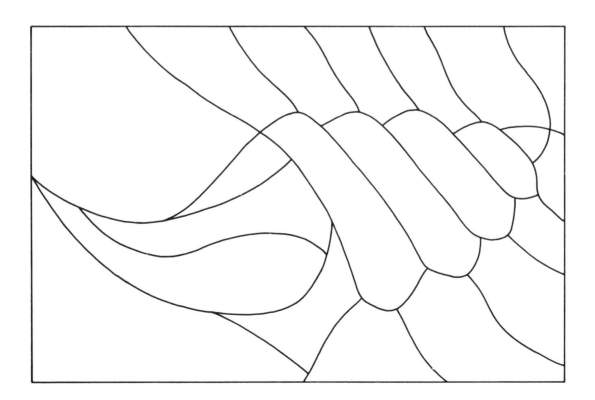

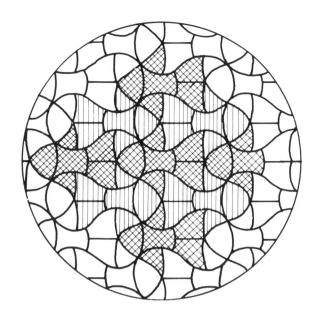

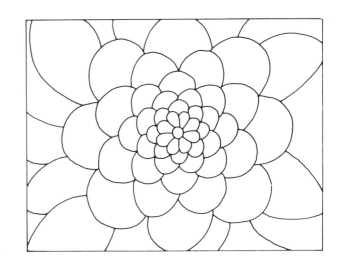

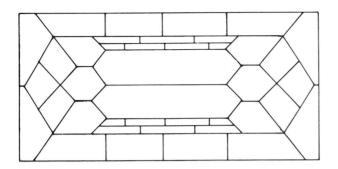

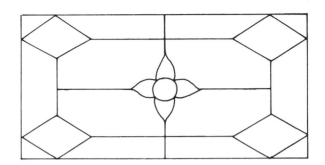

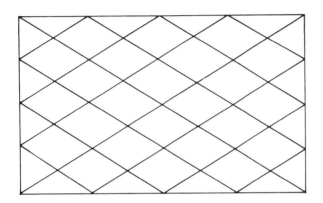

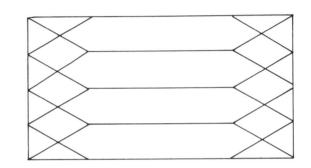

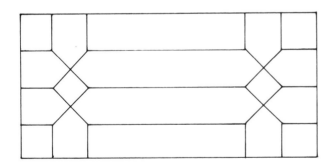

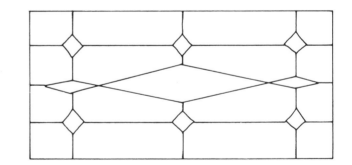

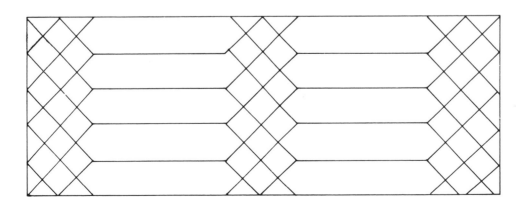

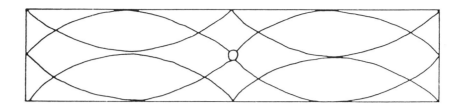

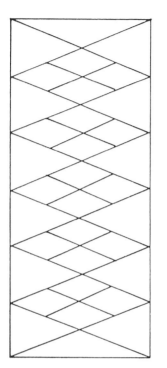
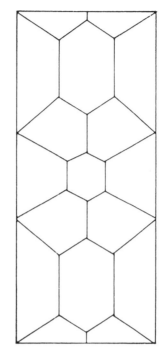
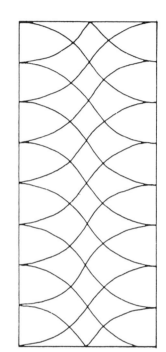

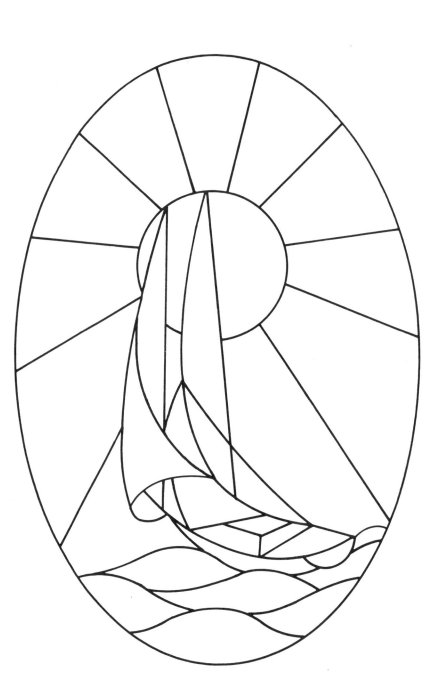

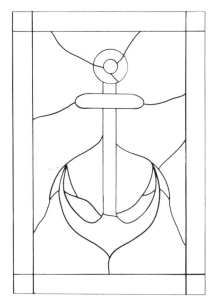